HOW SKINNER WAS WRONG

A Critical Remark on B. F. Skinner's
Radical Behaviorism

Daniel Grandinetti
Translated by Sabrina de Paula
2015

TABLE OF CONTENTS

PREFACE

This work is not a criticism to the behavioral psychotherapeutic method and the behavioral research method. Its target is Skinner's Radical Behaviorism as a Philosophy of Psychology. Consequently, the successes of the behavioral method in clinical psychology and scientific research are not evaluated herein. Instead, we discuss the philosophical premises of the internalism thesis used by Skinner as a reason to reject a priori psychological explanations in favor of behavioral explanations.

Skinner argued that psychological explanations are internalist, that is, they indicate the individual's inner and private motives such as desires, fears, and beliefs as the cause of his/her behavior. In the author's point of view, the private and inner nature of these causes implies two consequences: (1) They cannot be known directly by third parties and (2) they cannot be directly modified. The researcher or psychologist only notes the subjective motivations of third parties by inference or by verbal communication (when possible); and only succeeds in modifying them by changing environmental contingencies that affect or reinforce them. The manipulation of environmental contingencies not only modifies the subjective motivations conditioned or reinforced by them, it also alters the behavior that psychological theories indicate as its effect. Thus, for Skinner, both subjective motivations and the behavior listed in the psychological theories as cause and effect respectively are functions of environmental contingencies.

If psychological motivations are a function of the same environmental contingencies which influence and reinforce behavior, then there is no significant causal relationship between one thing and another. The causal role of subjective motivations in behavioral explanation is null. Subjective motivations are pseudo causes that explain nothing. And if one cannot observe them directly, rather infer them only, then they are no more than fanciful ideas. For the author, psychological explanations are explanatory fictions that speculate on subjective motives without a relevant causal role in behavior analysis.

Skinner classifies psychological explanations as vague, allusive, inaccurate, misleading, and ineffective. Behavior analysis, on the other hand, is accurate, determined, insightful and effective in behavioral control. Only behavior analysis provides its true causes. Consequently, focusing on subjective reasons, not allowing enough attention to be paid to environmental contingencies – the real causes of behavior in Skinner's thesis – results in their obfuscation and in the omission of the researcher or psychologist who simply fails to consider them.

This is the thesis being examined and criticized in the following pages. The conclusion (I can tell in advance) is a form of inversion of Skinner's position. I will show that subjective motivations are as objective as the environmental contingencies that appear in behavior analysis. I will further demonstrate that subjective motivations are the foundation of behavior analysis' objectivity, for they are that which gives it meaning and that, consequently, with the impossibility to infer the subjective sense of a behavior analysis, it itself becomes vague, allusive, inaccurate, misleading and ineffective in behavioral control.

1 - A Brief Exposition of the Theoretical and Methodological Principles of Radical Behaviorism

Why does an animal eat? The most common answer is: Because it is hungry. And why is it hungry? At this point, Skinner would answer: Because the animal has gone through a long period deprived from food. Thus, the explanatory chain for the animal behavior according to Skinner consists of three terms: (1) food deprivation; (2) the organic inner state of hunger; (3) the action of eating itself. (1) causes (2) which causes (3).

Of the three terms of this explanatory chain, only two are susceptible to observation or direct measurement. The time for which the animal was deprived of food can be measured, and its act of eating can be observed. The hunger experienced cannot be observed directly. It is inferred when we see an animal eating. If the animal eats, we think, it must be hungry. A different way to infer hunger, according to Skinner, is by weighing the animal before and after the deprivation period. A slight weight decrease could be a sign of hunger. Other inner state forms, the so-called "affective or emotional states", are more difficult to infer. But the problem Skinner sees in them has no relation with the ease or difficulty with which they are inferred; it is precisely the fact that they are the product of inferences that makes them problematic. Unlike variables (1) and (3), variable (2) is not susceptible to observation and direct measurement. This makes it impractical as a variable in an objective explanation. Possibly, we will have the means to detect affective states accurately in the future. But Skinner claims that (a) currently, it is not yet possible, and (b) even if possible, it would still be *unnecessary*.

The main thesis of Skinner's Behaviorism is that the variable (2) is unnecessary for a behavioral science. (1) can be causally connected to (3) without passing by or referencing (2). Thus, Skinner answers the question "Why does an animal eat?" with "Because it has spent a long time without eating". There is no need for an answer such as: "It spent a long time without eating, so it got hungry and it is now eating". Skinner considers his own answer simpler and therefore better. But its real advantage is not its simplicity. Competing answers to the same question are not necessarily composed of the three terms of the explanatory chain. As Skinner causally connected terms (1) and (3), it is also possible to relate only the terms (2) and (3). Why does an animal eat? It eats (3) *because* it is hungry (2). This is, as previously stated, the most common answer to that question.

The explanation "The animal eats because it is hungry" is as simple as "the animal eats because it spent a long time without eating." However, the second explanation tells us the causal condition of hunger: the deprivation of food. This condition can be directly observed and measured; therefore, it is subject to change. The inner hunger state cannot be directly changed. One can only change it by altering conditions which are its cause. While the explanation connecting (1) and (3) causally allows us to know the conditions by which we can *control* behavior, the explanation connecting (2) and (3) leaves our hands tied. What good is it being told the animal eats because it is hungry if this explanation does not indicate any condition that we could change to control the animal's eating behavior?

The chain formed by terms (1), (2) and (3) is effective to explain the unconditioned reflexes. No one needs to learn how to eat when he/she is hungry and there is food available. We do so naturally or "instinctively". It is also natural or instinctive for children to cry when they are hungry or going through another need or discomfort. But children can learn to cry even in the absence of these conditions, if the parents' promptitude in serving them when they cry provides positive consequences. Crying can make parents turn their attention to their children, hold them, give them affection, etc. Thus crying, once instinctive only under certain conditions, becomes *conditioned* by the positive consequences of the experience. The conditioned behavior can no longer be properly explained by variable (1). A new variable was added to the explanatory chain, (4) the consequences of (3) crying. If a child gets more attention by crying, this consequence of crying can be identified as the cause of crying every time that child wants attention. The "want to draw attention" can be described as "deprivation of attention" and count as variable (1) of the explanatory chain. But even if the child is deprived of his/her parents' attention, it is the history of parental thoughtful responses that will determine the cry for attention. After all, what good is for the child to cry, even though deprived of attention, if he/she "knows" that crying will not bring the desired attention?

The behavior modeled by experience in the way described above was named by Skinner *operant*, and the conditioning that underlies it *operant conditioning*. While the unconditioned behavior can be explained by the causal link between (1) and (3), an operant behavior is properly explained by the causal connection between (4) and (3). Both (1) and (4) are variables that can be changed, and altering these variables controls the behavior causally connected to them. Thus, Skinner feels authorized to defend his theory and methodology: As a behavior theory, behaviorism is the simplest of all, since it discards the variable (2), unnecessary in the explanatory chain. As a scientific methodology, behaviorism is the most efficient, since it is the only discipline that gets to behavior's root causes and does not make them obscure with speculative inferences about the organism's (2) inner states, whether affective or emotional. This is *Radical Behaviorism*, the science of behavior that explains it directly from its root causes.

Skinner's intention was to establish a science of behavior with the same objectivity standards of physical sciences. He distinguished the world "within the skin" from the world "outside the skin". The elements of a science of behavior had to be found in the world "outside the skin". The world "outside the skin" is the world shared by all; the world that can be described in the physical sciences' terminology. According to Skinner, Behavior's (1) initial conditions, its (4) consequences, positive - *reinforcements* - or negative - *punishments* -, are part of the world "outside the skin", and can be described by the natural sciences' terminology. On the other hand, the organism's (2) inner conditions are private. Only the organism itself has direct access to them. Such conditions are the variables "within the skin", and an external observer can only infer them. They are not part of the world shared by all and are not subject to direct observation by others.

Initially, one can note that the variables (1), (3) and (4) cannot always be described by the natural sciences' terminology. In Skinner's laboratory experiments with pigeons and rats, (1) and (3) could certainly be observed and described by this terminology. All behavior of rats and pigeons that interests the researcher is manifested by body movements, and the deprivation conditions to which they are subjected can be measured and described in scientific terminology. For human subjects however, the scenario changes. First, not all human behavior that interest Psychology is manifested in the world "outside the skin". People's (2) "inner life", contained in the privacy of their subjectivity, consists of key elements in a science that aims to cover behavior. Second, the (1) initial conditions and (4) consequences of human action can only be properly described in a subjective perspective. Words, for example, are means of reinforcement or punishment. Praise and criticism appear as important elements in Skinner's texts. But "praise" and "criticism" are not physical events and cannot be described by the of the natural sciences' terminology. The physical events that compose them are sound waves or vibrations of air molecules. Sound waves and vibrations of air molecules can only be described as "words" in the sphere of attribution of meaning or in the subjective sphere of the world "within the skin".

This criticism, however, is irrelevant. It only proves that Skinner's intention in establishing a science of behavior that could be fully described in the terminology of the natural sciences is unfounded. This may show a certain naivety or intellectual inability in Skinner, but is no argument against the fundamental principle of objectivity intended by Radical Behaviorism. Indeed, the substance of this claim to objectivity is the allegation that behavior can be explained and controlled by an analysis that causally relates variables (1) and (3) or (4) and (3). In other words, Skinner's claim to objectivity lies in the allegation that the knowledge of the subject's (2) affective or organic states *qua* inner affective or organic states is unnecessary for behavior explanation and control. The knowledge of inner (2) affective or organic states can help clarify the relationship between (1) and (3) or (4) and (3); but showing no significant cause in the explanation of (3) behavior, it is unnecessary in its control.

Although words cannot be described in scientific terminology, they are part of public domain. Words are spoken by people; and, to the extent that someone's words reinforce or extinguish another person's behavior, they are variables which can be changed through dialogue and communication. Similarly, instead of taking a client's inner life as the (2) variable of inner affective or organic states that figures in some non-behavioral explanations (so claims Skinner) as the cause of (3) behavior, we can take it as their own (3) behavior to be explained. Under these conditions, the client can talk openly to the analyst about his/her (3) "private behavior", giving the analyst the opportunity to investigate the variables (1) and (4) that control this behavior and the possibilities to modify them. In short, Radical Behaviorism's claim to objectivity is the allegation that (2) inner affective and organic states, that is, all that is commonly called "subjectivity", have no causal role in explaining and controlling behavior, and such states enter a behavioral science only in the condition of (3) behavior that needs to be explained. When critics of Radical Behaviorism claim that behavior analysis ignores subjectivity, its advocates respond that they are wrong and affirm that Radical Behaviorism sees our thoughts, ideas, and emotions as behaviors or as something to be explained by a behavioral science. It seems as though Skinner is immune to criticism.

2 - Behavioral Analysis is not Explanatory

Before we render a definitive verdict, let us imagine the following situation: A group of people are invited to visit a laboratory and are presented with a mouse eagerly devouring its food. They are given the following explanation: "This mouse went two whole days without food. Moments ago, the first time in two days, the mouse was given a bit of food. The time the mouse spent deprived of food is the cause of it be eating now". Then, they are asked these two questions:

a) Do you agree with this explanation?

b) Why?

I have not tried this experiment. But I believe that in almost all cases the answers would be, respectively:

a) Yes.

b) Because the mouse was hungry.

The allegation that (1) the time deprived of food is the cause of (3) the act of eating is based on the fact that (3) is a dependent variable of (1) and that the changes in (1) can control (3). However, this experimental evidence is not sufficient to justify the allegation that the establishment of the causal relationship between (1) and (3) composes an explanation of (3). Any explanation must be intelligible. If not intelligible, nothing is explained. The conditions of intelligibility are not connected to the ability of individual understanding. The intelligible explanation includes the necessary conditions to make itself understood, leaving to the individual the task of understanding it.

The intelligibility of an explanation is linked to the fact that it is intuitive. However, an explanation may initially seem counterintuitive and later reveal itself intuitive through individual effort. In turn, although some explanations seem intuitive at first, they may reveal themselves counterintuitive after subsequent analysis.

Newton's Mechanics revealed relationships that seemed counterintuitive at first; very differently from Aristotle's Physics, for instance, that was more in accordance with the way nature seems to operate at first glance. However, as much as the equation $f = m.a$ may seem counterintuitive at a first glance, it contains every condition to become intuitive. This is an intelligible explanation. The correct understanding of the relations among force, mass, and acceleration established by the equation is enough to make it intuitive. Understanding the formula requires no inference of variables other than those that compose it. The formula thus schematized truly explains the causal relations which it aims to explain.

Things are different for the causal link established by Skinner between (1) deprivation of food and (3) the act of eating. In fact, the case of behaviorist explanations is exactly opposite to Newton's explanations. That (1) deprivation of food is the cause of (3) eating seems clear and intuitive at first. However, the conditions for its intelligibility are not strictly contained in the relationship between (1) and (3). The causal relationship between (1) and (3) only becomes understandable if (2) the mouse's hunger is inferred from the relationship itself. The strict causal relationship between (1) and (3) is counterintuitive. What makes it intuitive is the inference that, when (1) deprived of food, the mouse (2) got hungry. For the behaviorist explanation to become truly explanatory, we must infer from it a variable that is not present. The inference is implicitly performed by the interlocutor who acknowledges the explanation, and from this inference rises the illusion that the so formulated explanation is intuitive, genuinely explanatory and objective.

In understanding Newton's formula, a high school student makes it intelligible scrutinizing the relations among force, mass, and acceleration. These are the only three variables needed so that the formula becomes explanatory. In understanding Skinner's formula, a Psychology student makes it intelligible by inferring a variable not given by it. The formula, by itself, does not contain the variables needed in order to become explanatory. Furthermore, the variable inferred in the understanding of Skinner's formula is subjective. The *sine qua non* condition for the intelligibility of behavioral formulas is the (2) subjective variable which Skinner claimed to be unnecessary for the explanation of behavior. Formulas that establish a causal relationship between (2) hunger and (3) the act of eating are intuitive, intelligible, and explanatory. But the behaviorist formulas that establish a causal relationship between (1) and (3) are counterintuitive, unintelligible, and non-explanatory, except when the variable (2) can be inferred by them. Thus (2) is the *sine qua non* condition for the causality between (1) and (3) to be effectively causal; for if the mouse does not get hungry, the (1) food deprivation time will never be the cause of (3) eating. (2) is the *sine qua non* condition for any behavioral or psychological explanation to acquire real explanatory value. It is because of (2) that (1) is the cause of (3). Skinner could not eliminate (2) from behavioral explanations. Instead, he relegated it to the implicit variable status. And that which was implicit turned out to be essential.

If what is essential in behaviorist explanations is the (2) subjective variable that lies implicit in them, behavioral explanations are fundamentally subjective. Unlike Physics' formulas which become intelligible simply by analyzing the objective variables they provide, behaviorist formulas only become intelligible when we add to their analysis the variable (2), which is subjective and lies implicit in them.

Skinner relied on the premise that affection, emotions, and thoughts are inner or private variables, and therefore could not be observed directly by third parties. Inner variables can only be inferred. According to Skinner, this condition compromised the objectivity of any psychological theory. In order for Psychology to become objective, it should only comprise elements of the world "outside the skin", as these are shared by all and are not enclosed in anyone's private world. In doing so, Skinner's intention was to bring objectivity into Psychology, in both senses of the word: Limiting psychological explanations to objective elements only – explanations regarding the object, in other words, the environment, never the subject - giving them the absolute and universal form that would make behavior predictable - since they would not be subject neither to the indeterminacy of inferences about (2) inner variables nor to interpretative elaboration of others.

But the inference which Skinner wanted to eliminate from behavior analysis is exactly what gives it meaning. Skinner did not eliminate the inference of (2) inner variables; he only worked out a way to talk about them without making explicit reference to them. It's like someone who learns to talk about sex without referring explicitly to sexuality, leaving implicit the sexual meaning he/she wants to convey. When the behaviorist says that (1) deprivation led the mouse to (3) the act of ingesting food, the meaning being communicated implicitly is: The mouse got hungry. And both the behaviorist and his interlocutor grasp this meaning, although neither of them verbalize or stop to think about it.

The objectivity achieved by Radical Behaviorism is metaphorical. The causal relationship of objective elements is explicitly talked about, but the significance of the relationship remains given by implicit psychological concepts. The objective relationship contains a subjective sense. The relationships among variables in Physics, in turn, are objective and do not contain any implicit subjective meaning; they consist of objective relations with objective meaning.

The same criticism applied to the relationship between (1) and (3) also applies to the relationship between (4) and (3). When a behaviorist says, for example, that a parent reinforces his daughter's obedient behavior by giving her candy, behind the concept of (4) reinforcement a whole (2) psychology is implied that infers the child's taste for sweets, the ever vivid desire for them – although this desire might be sometimes dormant - the satisfaction caused by eating candy, etc. The reinforcement concept is metaphorical. It is not even objective in the sense of being "object-related". There is no object or physical relationship that can be called "behavioral reinforcement". "Behavioral reinforcement" is a concept devoid of objective meaning. And if some behaviorist tries to make it objective by revealing the (2) organic phenomena that mediate the relationship between (4) maintainer stimulus and (3) response, it will be an attack against Radical Behaviorism's deepest foundation: the behaviorist will be complementing the relationship between (4) reinforcement and (3) behavior with the description of (2) an inner-organic non-behavioral variable and admitting, between the lines, that the investigation of behavioral variables alone is not enough to either give objectivity to the analysis of behavior nor to make it explanatory.

Skinner believed that the variable (2) is internal, that is, a component of the world "within the skin". Whether the description of this variable is made in biological or psychological terms, the author's criticism remains the same. Inasmuch as the variable (2) is explanatory, it is not behavioral. To make it behavioral, one needs to define it as (3) behavior, or as part of what must be explained. In this case, it ceases performing the function of variable (2) and starts performing the function of variable (3). If the (2) mouse's hunger ceases to perform an explanatory function in the relationship between (1) deprivation and (3) the act of eating and turns into the (3) behavior to be explained by (1) deprivation, it becomes behavioral and an object of behavior analysis.

Generally, the assumption that (1) long fasting led someone to (3) get hungry is immediately intuitive and needs no further explanation. Things get a bit complicated if we ask why. Why does fasting for a long time cause hunger? The causal link between "fasting" and "hunger" becomes intuitive by habit. Historically, we have become used to feeling hungry when fasting for a long time and to see the same happening to others. But if we are disciplined enough to leave aside the strong impressions of habit and seriously question ourselves about the meaning of this causal relationship, we may come to the conclusion that it is not as intuitive and explanatory as we thought it was and, in fact, its meaning is not at all obvious.

If we seek for a causality or subjective condition for hunger instead of an environmental condition (deprivation), we will have a much deeper understanding of the phenomenon. If we find a psychological causality for hunger, we will come a little closer to the true objectivity of psychology. If the (2) subjective variable no longer performs an explanatory function and acquires a (3) behavioral function, and if we relate it to a (1) subjective variable instead of relating it to an (1) environmental variable, that does not mean that the relationship between (1) subjective and (3) subjective makes it unnecessary to analyze variable (2), also subjective, which is interpolated in it and gives it meaning. Psychological theories are the product of inquiries about the variable (2) which gives meaning to the relationship between (1) and (3). The more subjective variables (1) and (3) are, the more objective will be the psychological theory that results from the analysis of the variable (2) which gives it meaning. For the more subjective the psychological theory is, the smaller will be the specific environmental conditions which limit their application and therefore, the larger will be the number of cases covered by it. The psychological theory that achieves universality will be totally objective.

Behavior analysts dodge the critics who accuse Radical Behaviorism of disregarding the subjectivity answering that the behaviorist theory recognizes subjectivity as part of what must be explained. This response distorts the meaning of that criticism. Obviously, critics accuse Radical Behaviorism of disregarding the subjectivity as part of the explanation, for which they are absolutely correct.

Behaviorists disregard the explanatory function of subjectivity. They assume that the occupation with the explanatory meaning of variable (2) leads the analysis of (1) and (3) to the inner environment "within the skin", pushing it away from the initial environmental conditions which, according to them, are the true causes of behavior. They fail to understand that a deep study of variable (2) produces psychological theories and that psychological theories do not relate to the way the "inner mind" works. Instead, they build a subjective perspective in which the relationship between the (1) environmental conditions and (3) the behavior can be interpreted.

Behaviorists do not analyze the explanatory meaning of variable (2). Consequently, Radical Behaviorism does not present a psychological theory; it presents us with a critical philosophy of Psychology and a methodology of research and analysis of behavior. But the psychological theory behaviorists refuse to elaborate is implicit in every behavior analysis they perform. The premise "the mouse got hungry because it was deprived of food" is a psychological explanation and refers to a general psychological theory that relates (3) hunger as behavior and the (1) deprivation as a contingency that conditions it: The (1) deprivation is the cause of (3) hunger. Although this is not a complete psychological theory that relates a subjective variable (1) to a subjective variable (3), this theory is what gives meaning to the causal relationship between (1) deprivation and (3) the mouse's act of eating. The whole psychological meaning implicit in the case of a father reinforcing his daughter's obedient behavior also refers to a general psychological theory implicit in behavioral analysis. Behaviorists reject all psychological theory, yet their analysis is not exempt from it. However, since the behavioral psychological theory stays implicit, it does not develop, does not reach deeper, and remains indefinitely in the embryonic stage. One of the arguments most frequently used by behaviorists in favor of Radical Behaviorism is one that calls for "Occam's Razor": The behaviorist theory is the best because, by eliminating the variable (2) from the explanation, it becomes simpler than its competitors. However, since the behaviorist does not eliminate variable (2) from the analysis, leaving it only implicit, underlying and stagnant in its incipient form, the simplicity of behavioral analysis confuses itself with superficiality.

Psychological theories are implicit in behaviorist explanations. That is enough to invalidate Radical Behaviorism as an explanatory theory of behavior. In the following pages, I will demonstrate the theory is also invalid in its pretenses to control behavior.

A simple example can illustrate how essential psychological theories are in making the analysis of behavior intelligible. In clinical practice, it is quite common to receive clients who are aware of the (1) initial conditions that make them (3) act in such a way and the (4) consequences that have historically preserved this pattern of behavior. However, they come to us disoriented, because they do not understand why. It is not necessary to put them through a behavior analysis; they have done the analysis themselves. These clients are perfectly capable of causally relating (1) and (3) and (4) and (3). Still, such causal relationships do not make sense to them. The meaning of variable (2) must be clarified so that the causal relationships already known by them become intelligible. Psychological theory underlies the analysis of variable (2) which makes the relationship between (1), (3), and (4) intelligible and explanatory. In the absence of such analysis, these relationships reveal themselves counterintuitive, unintelligible and pseudo-explanatory. The behaviorist might still reply: "It does not matter that these relationships are not explanatory. What matters is that they make us know the variables that control behavior". I believe that the clients in question would disagree with this statement. Indeed, for them, what needs to be controlled in the first place is the anguish and anxiety of not feeling in control of their own actions. They have no knowledge of the (2) subjective variable which gives their behavior meaning; therefore, they do not feel they are the performers of their own actions. They cannot modify the known variables if they do not understand the meaning of their relationship. Understanding the relationships among variables (1), (3) and (4) is essential to any directive action that aims to change them. Therefore, behavior control requires the analysis of variable (2). This is required both so that the individuals will properly feel as owners of their actions and so that the client or the psychotherapist can take any directive action in modifying variables (1) and (4) which control the client's (3) behavior.

Whenever a behaviorist intervenes directly by modifying variables (1) and (4) which control (3) the client's behavior, he/she acts according to the implicit analysis of the (2) subjective variable. Although the behaviorist's psychological theory remains embryonic, rudimentary and rustic, it is still the foundation of all behavioral analysis performed by him/her. What is decisive in behavior analysis is neither the historical analysis of variables (1) and (4) nor the establishment of causal relationships between (1) and (3) or (4) and (3). The determinant factor in behavior analysis is the analyst's understanding of these relationships, and this understanding can only be achieved through the inferential analysis of the (2) subjective variable. This inference presupposes some kind of psychological theory. The psychological theory is the foundation of their psychotherapeutic successes, not mere analysis of behavior.

Although many successes are attributed to behavioral therapy, they serve as no evidence of the behavioral theory's validity as a practice of behavior control. Ultimately, if the inferential analysis of (2) the subjective variable is what underlies the behaviorist's psychotherapeutic actions, the success of behavioral therapy can be precisely used as evidence of the failure of Skinner's pretenses in producing an objective method of behavior control. It can be taken as a strong argument that the analysis of the (2) subjective variable is essential for Psychology, both as theory and as practice.

3 - Skinner and his Critique of Psychoanalysis

Skinner developed the Radical Behaviorism theory as a critical Philosophy of Psychology. According to the author, traditional Psychology was full of "explanatory fictions". By "explanatory fictions", he meant explanations that drifted away from the search for causality in environmental conditions and got lost in speculative inferences about states of affairs that we cannot observe directly. Traditional Psychology was founded in explanatory fictions because its explanations were *internalist*. Skinner defines as "internalism" all explanation patterns that seek for the causes of behavior within the organism. For Skinner, the living organism is a complicated system that behaves in complicated ways. Because of its unpredictability, the traditional procedure has been to seek an "inner determinant" to explain it; something that, throughout history, has been called the "demon", "homunculus" or "personality". This inner determinant would be able to make spontaneous changes in the course of behavior or to originate behavior on its own. For Skinner, psychoanalytic theory is a form of "internalism".

Skinner does not accuse Freud of sketching an inner determinant able to spontaneously originate behavior. He claims that Freud was a complete deterministic who had accepted the task of explaining the mental apparatus behavior. In Skinner's view, Freud explained the mental dynamics by giving it external environmental causes. Thus, Freud's causal relations were represented, according to Skinner, by a series of three events or terms: (1) Some environmental condition, usually located at the beginning of the individual's life, produces an (2) effect on the inner mental apparatus, and this effect, processed along by inner mental causes produces (3) the current behavior or symptom. For Skinner, Freud did not use the inner mental apparatus to explain spontaneity or whim. Instead, he used it to fill the space-time gap between the (1) environmental condition or stimulus and the (3) behavior or response.

Skinner explains behavior through the "stimulus-response-consequence" model. The body reacts to the (1) environmental or stimulus condition with (3) behavior or response and the (4) positive or negative consequence of this behavior determines whether it will be selected and developed or extinguished. Skinner called this process "shaping" behavior. He argues that Freud would have imposed a (2) mental apparatus inside the organism to mediate between (1) and (3). This mental apparatus, in addition to being superfluous and unnecessary, in

Skinner's opinion, contributes autonomously and independently of any influences or environmental conditions with its own causalities in processing stimulus into responses. One of the great problems of establishing an (2) inner mental apparatus to mediate between (1) stimulus and (3) response is, in Skinner's view, the difficulty of observation of the mental life. He points out as one of Freud's merits the conclusion that not everything in our inner mental life is directly accessible to observation, and that many mental events are necessarily inferred. But he criticizes Freud for not taking the next step and coming to the conclusion that *all* mental events, conscious or unconscious, are the product of inferences: mental events are not facts, but inferences from facts. Facts are (3) reactions of the organism to (1) environmental conditions. Skinner argues that the individual, rather than reacting to an (2) inner experience (1) from the environment, reacts directly to the environment itself. Thus, he believes to be eliminating the bifurcation between physical and mental nature, solving the mind-body dualism. Besides involving the mind-body dualism, the splitting of nature in "physical" and "mental" would also bring about difficulties in explaining the psychotherapeutic action. For Skinner, the psychotherapist acts on the individual, through physical means manipulating variables that occupy the variable (1) in the explanatory chain. But how could material causalities influence the psychism? This is the old issue about the interaction between physical and mental elements.

Skinner's criticism draws its strength from the comparison he makes between the consequences of accepting the premise of an inner intermediate mental apparatus and the consequences of the premise defended by him. In the author's position, Freud would have pointed strikingly to the importance of (1) environmental conditions in psychoanalytic explanations. Indeed, childhood traumas, relationship nuances between the child and his/her parents and everyday events constitute (1) important causal factors in psychoanalytic explanations. These are the facts of the individual's life which Skinner called "environmental conditions", and the (1) environmental conditions occupy the first term in Freud's causal chain without which the (3) symptoms, object of study in psychoanalytic theory, would not exist. Well, for Skinner, the (1) individual's life facts are lost and obscured when represented in the (2) mental life. For instance, Skinner believes the (1) punishment for sexual behavior in childhood results, undoubtedly, in the (2) modification of the organism. When the modifications of the organism are described as changes in the inner mental apparatus and when the analysis focuses on the dynamics of these changes, it combines, transforms, and processes the (1) punishment experiences within the (2) mental apparatus in conscious and unconscious states of anxiety and guilt. In the subjectivation of the (1) punishment experiences, they are described in the form of a (2) dynamics between anxiety and guilt, which obscures its specific details. Therefore, when some unusual features of the (3) adult sexual behavior are attributed to (2) anxiety and guilt, many details of the relationship between the (1) act of punishment and the (3) sexual behavior are lost; details that would have been clarified if the (3) sexual behavior had been directly related to the (1) act of punishment and not to the (2) mental processing that mediated the two things.

Skinner gives us a concrete example from Freud's life story. The author reports that as a child, Freud lost a younger brother and his playmate was replaced by another child who, although stronger and older than him, was his nephew. Later, Freud allegedly said that the rivalry which aroused from the relationship with his nephew would have had great impact on his theories and adult relationships. Skinner argues that classifying as (2) "rivalry in family" the (1) set of circumstances concerning the relationship between Freud and his nephew obscures the many properties of this family relationship. In a science of behavior, on the contrary, each one of the characteristics in that relationship would be distinguished and studied as an (1) independent variable. Similarly, to argue that such (1) properties resulted in (2) conscious or unconscious aggressive tendencies and guilt feelings also means giving them a misrepresentation. An emphasis on (3) behavior would lead us to inquire about (1) other circumstances in these childhood episodes. In short, Skinner claims that causally connecting the (1) environmental conditions to (2) mental processes, and mental processes to the (3) symptom or behavior prevents the study of the relationship between (1) and (3) from going further. Skinner lists a series of questions that would be raised by a behavioral approach; questions that are not raised in similar cases in a psychoanalytic approach, he suggests. What did the young Freud learn to do to get his parents' attention in these difficult circumstances? Did he exaggerate some disease? Did he feign illness? Did he explicitly show some behavior that would bring him approval? Does that behavior belong to the field of physical or intellectual abilities? Did he hit or hurt other children? Did he learn to tease them and hurt them verbally? Was he punished for it and, if so, did he find other forms of behavior that had the same harmful effect, but were immune to punishment?

Skinner explains the behavior in terms of the relationship between organism and environment; a physical relationship between two entities whose nature can be described by the natural sciences: While the organism is biological, the environment is physical and chemical. Skinner accuses Freud of having situated between the organism and the environment a world of mental nature whose elements and forces cannot be described by the natural sciences. This mental world, located inside the organism, gives us the "inner experience" of the environment that exists externally. According to the author, when (1) environmental conditions are internalized and described as (2) elements and forces of a mental nature, this transformation not only obscures the (1) environmental conditions which are the real causes of behavior, it also causes them to be lost completely. He then cleverly concludes that in (2) mental elements and forces the (1) true causes of behavior are absent, and explanations that consider them causal factors of human actions are nothing but "explanatory fictions", which the author pejoratively called "fabrications". Moreover, if in the study of the inner experience of the environment, the (2) resulting mental forces and elements completely lose connection with the (1) environmental conditions which Freud postulated as the cause of (2) subsequent mental processes, the causal relationship between (1) environmental conditions and (2) mental life becomes completely inappropriate. In practice, what we have are desires, fears, and beliefs; an entire mental life that is pure speculation after all and that would alone explain (3) behavior without any reference to (1) environment conditions when used in psychological theories. This is the (2) "Initiator self" or that immaterial soul or mind that spontaneously generates ideas, feelings, and beliefs and that, *per se*, determines (3) behavior. Therefore, the (2) psychoanalytic mental apparatus, having no link with the (1) real causes of (3) behavior, and only based on inference, would be no more than a "castle in the sky". Skinner starts off by ridding Freud of the charges for having used the (2) inner mental apparatus to spontaneously explain (3) behavior and concludes later that, after all, that is precisely what psychoanalytic theory ends up doing.

4 - Elucidating Skinner's Caricature about Psychoanalysis

It is necessary to elucidate the errors in Skinner's critique on Psychoanalysis. The mental apparatus does not (2) internally represent the (1) external environment. When (3) behavior is explained in a (2) mental perspective, we must call it *experience*. Mentalist Psychologies have experience as their object of study. And when it comes to experience, there is no difference between (1) environmental conditions and (2) mental life conditions. For Psychoanalysis, an experience can be conscious or unconscious. Therefore, when Psychoanalysis approaches conscious and unconscious mental elements, it is not referring to a dynamics of (2) inner forces; it refers to dimensions of our being-in-the-world that are conscious or unconscious. In other words, a conscious or unconscious desire is not something that exists "only within our mind"; it exists as the subject's relation to the world, an affectionate relationship. Desires, intentions, and beliefs are not "things" that exist within us, inaccessible to sunlight; they are relations with the world and its objects.

For this reason, the dualism issue raised by Skinner, that is, the way (1) physical stimuli can determine effects on the (2) mental apparatus is a false problem. The psychotherapist's words, as well as all other environmental stimuli, are objects of the experience world, and their influences on the patient can also be described as mental nature elements or forces.

Every little nuance, property or feature of the relationship between the subject and the world can be described in the mentalist language. A given affection is conscious, obviously, when the subject is aware of it in his/her relation with the object. It is unconscious when the subject is not aware of it in object relation. This does not mean that the unconscious affection exists behind the conscious affection. It means only that, in the analysis of the conscious relationship between subject and object, a different type of relationship – hitherto unnoticed by the subject – appeared as determinant. This is what is implied when, in the psychoanalytic process, the analyst infers that an unconscious desire lies in the client's conscious fear, or that an unconscious desire lies in the conscious desire. The unconscious desire in an object relation often reveals itself, undisguised, in the conscious desire for another object. Any behavior analyst points out to his/her clients the (4) environmental conditions that have been reinforcing the (3) unwanted behavior without them noticing it. There would be no behavior analysis if the analyst did not work this way. The psychoanalyst performs the same work in a different language.

Skinner's criticism to mentalism is based on the ontology he adopted. This ontology describes the world divided into two distinct environments, each of them constituted of their own forces: A (2) world within the skin and a (1) world outside the skin. For Skinner, the mentalist vocabulary describes the (2) world within the skin which is private and inaccessible to observation by others. Consequently, in order for Psychology to become objective, it would have to be founded on the observation of operative forces in the (1) world outside the skin, and these forces would have to be described in the appropriate vocabulary, that of the natural sciences. However, as we have seen, the causal description between (1) environmental conditions and (3) behavior only makes sense when its meaning is subjective. The subjective meaning of relations between the subject and the world is what composes mentalism. "Mentalist" is all psychology or philosophy that gives a subjective meaning to the relationship between the subject and the world. To give this relationship a subjective meaning, mentalism describes it in the mentalist or psychological vocabulary. "Desire", "intention", "belief", etc., are expressions that reflect the subjective meaning of the relationship between the subject and the world, the only meaning able to make sense of that relationship. Hence, mentalism does not necessarily need to have as a premise the existence of a mind within the subject. Skinner's criticism which restricts the mentalist vocabulary to the description of an inner world, private and inaccessible to observation by others is, therefore, wrong.

But is it not true that Freud left us two mental topics in which he postulated consciousness, the unconscious, the ego, the id and the superego as instances or mind compartments? And is it not true, that it would be absurd to claim that these topics do not refer to a mind located within the subject? All this is true. But it is also true that Freud built his topics on the account of "auxiliary concepts" for the explanation of objective phenomena. He had in mind the same situation of the natural sciences which speculate about unobservable realities to assist the explanations of physical phenomena. Examples of speculative and hypothetical auxiliary concepts include the atom, the subatomic elements and the forces acting in their interaction, gravity and the space-time curvature. Although impossible to observe, for instance, the atom and the forces governing the relationships between its parts, the atomic model helps us to explain several observable physical phenomena. Similarly, "desire", "intention", "belief", etc. are types of relationship between the subject and the world which, in addition to being experienced in us by ourselves, are also observable, for example, in patients in psychotherapy. And because the explanation given to them by Freud is complex and abstract, he used hypothetical mental topics to make it graphically intuitive and easier to understand. In the course of Psychoanalysis' development, it is even possible that Freud let himself be enchanted by the beauty of the theoretical edifice he was building, and it is also possible that Freud sometimes would treat this edifice as something beyond a simple auxiliary and hypothetical scheme. Freud was not immune to error. However, nothing justifies the use Skinner made of these mistakes. Indeed, Skinner used Freud's mistakes to justify his own mistakes, which were even greater.

If we deal subjectively with the relationships between (1) environmental conditions and (3) behavior and describe them as relations between (2) elements and mental forces, we would not be compromising the complexity of the properties in this relationship in any way. But Skinner assumes that psychoanalytic explanations run out in the study of (2) causalities within the organism which, in addition to being inferential and speculative, cut the links between the subject and the world, obscuring the relationship between (1) environmental conditions and (3) behavior. To justify his point of view, he gives us a very particular reading of how psychoanalytic explanations are engendered. He claims that when the (4) result of (3) Freud's relations with (1) his nephew was described as effects on (2) aggressive tendencies and guilt feelings, many details of this relationship were lost. So when the (3) later adult behavior is related to these (2) mental elements and forces, the resulting explanation becomes empty and lacks all the details (briefly listed above) which, according to Skinner, would be investigated on a behavior analysis. To go straight to the point, it suffices to say that the same criticism could be raised against the analysis of behavior if a similar opaque reading of the behaviorist theory were to be made by us. A psychoanalyst could raise the following questions on Freud's case: Was Freud's relationship with his nephew guided by affective ambivalence? Could it be that while he loved him as playmate and admired him for being older, Freud's own physical inferiority in relation to his nephew bothered him considering that, theoretically, an uncle must be older and stronger than his nephew? Besides, was he not a nephew who was coming to replace Freud's younger brother? But what right did he have to do that, or how could he have the simple intention of replacing his brother? Is it not possible that, while he loved his nephew as a new brother, young Freud thought he would be thus betraying his dead brother? What are the consequences of this guilt feeling on Freud's aggressive tendencies – which probably already existed because of a fight for hierarchy? Did he openly express his aggressiveness? If so, did he feel again guilty about it or did he feel relieved? If not, how did he deal with the unmanifested aggression? Repressing it? Rationalizing it in view of religious premises? Taking it out on someone else? There is indeed an indefinite number of questions that can be raised about this story. In light of this, would it not seem too crude and opaque if, in the case of a neurotic symptom appearing in adulthood, we were to affirm simply that its cause was the "reinforcing" of some behaviors during childhood rather than causally relating it to the psychic complex described above? What would we be explaining with this? The answer is very simple: We would not be explaining anything at all!

Indeed, "reinforcement" is a general term that only acquires explanatory meaning of particular facts when applied to an individual's life circumstances. Similarly, Psychoanalysis provides us with a psychological theory that, as any theory, has a general, universal and unspecified nature. Taken in its "theory" form, it also does not explain anything, unless in an equally general, universal and unspecified way. For psychoanalytic theory to be able to explain individual behavior, it must be applied to the wide range of circumstances and particularities of *that* individual's life. In this sense, there is a big difference between theory and explanation. Skinner took general psychoanalytic theory and used it to try to explain the rich nuances of individual behavior without applying it to any particular case. And I say this as I collude with Skinner, since "aggressive tendencies and guilt feelings" do not compose psychoanalytic theory whatsoever. Obviously, after taking psychoanalytic theory in such a distorted, simplified and reduced way and using it to explain individual behavior, Skinner's conclusion could not have been different: In psychoanalytic explanations, the entire complexity of the relationships between organism and environment is obscured and lost. Only Radical Behaviorism provides us with a model in which the true causes of behavior can be properly distinguished, considered, and understood. A nice pamphlet text in defense of the superiority of Radical Behaviorism.

5 - The Misuse of Evolutionism by Radical Behaviorism

Behavior analysis does not provide an answer to why a given behavior has been emitted. The reason why the mouse eats after being deprived of food is "because he got hungry", but Radical Behaviorism denies the explanatory validity of that answer. Behavior analysis investigates the (4) history of reinforcements and punishments of a (3) behavior and the (1) initial conditions in which it is issued. In short, it investigates the (1) conditions that trigger the behavior and (4) the conditions that shape that behavior.

According to behavioral terminology, the mouse that (3) eats after (1) having been deprived of food issues a reflective or unconditioned behavior. On the other hand, the child who (3) cries, not for being (1) deprived of food, but because crying (4) draws his or her parents' attention, issues a conditioned behavior called "operant". In the case of operant behavior, behavior analysis does not seek for causes only in the (1) initial conditions, but also and mainly in the (4) consequences, that is, the child (3) cries because in past occasions when he/she (2) was hungry and (3) cried, (4) he/she received extra attention from his/her parents. Thus, the child may (3) cry, even not being (2) hungry, only to (4) receive more attention. Under these conditions, the analytical question "why does the child (3) cry" is answered with "to (4) get more attention".

Evidently, this answer still does not explain why the child wants more attention; this response could only be provided by a psychological explanation. However, it places Radical Behaviorism on the same track by which it was distinguished from the earlier forms of behaviorism, especially that of Watson's: for Radical Behaviorism, most behavioral issues that are important to Psychology should not be explained by (1) initial or triggering conditions but by the (4) history of their positive or negative consequences.

According to Radical Behaviorism, (3) behavior can be explained by the analysis of (4) its positive or negative consequences. Positive consequences reinforce it; negative consequences tend to extinguish it. Reinforced behavior shows increased frequency of future emissions; punished behavior has reduced frequency of future emissions. Thus reinforced behavior tends to be selected within the behavioral repertoire of an organism, while punished behavior tends to be eliminated.

Skinner adopts Darwin's selectionist model to explain how the (4) history of reinforcements and punishments explains (3) behavior. But obviously, all behavior has a first emission which occurred without any historical precedence. In this case, (3) behavior should be explained by its (1) initial conditions. As we have seen, the direct causal relationship between (1) and (3) is not explanatory. It only becomes explanatory through the meaning acquired from a (2) psychological analysis. Radical Behaviorism acknowledges the senselessness of this relationship because, in fact, it tries to make some sense of it. However, since it cannot explicitly seek for meaning in a psychological theory, it seeks for meaning in evolutionism. Hence, when asked "why does the mouse (3) eat after being (1) deprived of food", the behavior analyst will say that the mouse (3) eats (1) under these conditions because over time, during the evolution of species, the act of eating as a result of food deprivation proved to have been adapted to environmental conditions, passed through the sieve of natural selection and was genetically transmitted to future generations.

In short, for Radical Behaviorism, both the (3) behavior first emitted and the reflective and unconditioned behavior is explained by (1) environmental conditions that triggered it and by phylogenetic heritage. Our organism is phylogenetically programmed to (3) behave in certain ways in (1) specific contexts. When properly (1) stimulated by the appropriate context, the (3) corresponding behavior is emitted, according to the phylogenetically inherited programming.

Evolutionary reasons are a necessary evil to a psychology that gave up the psychological theories. As a whole, evolutionary reasons constitute a theory called "Evolutionary Psychology" which is unsuitable for explaining individual cases. General and universal Psychological theory acquires a particular shape when applied to individual cases. Thus, a psychological theory may acquire as many particular shapes as are the individuals to whom it applies. When individualized, a psychological theory becomes the explanation of that particular behavior being analyzed. Evolutionary Psychology maintains its general and universal shape when applied to any individual. It is never particularized. Therefore, for Radical Behaviorism, Evolutionary Psychology is a necessary evil, but only when strictly necessary. Because Radical Behaviorism's need for evolutionary explanations is restricted to cases where the meaning of behavior, its "reason" cannot be given implicitly in a behavioral variable. This is both the case of the first emitted behavior and the case of reflective and unconditioned behavior.

The meaning of behavior is its intent, and the clarification of its intent explains behavior itself. When the mouse (3) eats on the first opportunity after being (1) deprived of food, the meaning of this behavior is given by (2) hunger; its explanation can be "the mouse (3) eats because it is (2) hungry". But the explanation in precise terms should be "the mouse (3) ate to *quench* its (2) hunger". "Quenching the hunger" is the pursuit of satiety, which is nothing more than the satisfaction or pleasure that eliminates a need. The ultimate intent of the (3) mouse's behavior, therefore, is (2) satisfaction. All forms of behavior, even those which are first emitted, have some form of satisfaction as their ultimate intent. The explanation which clarifies the (2) satisfaction connected to (3) all forms of behavior is the objective to be achieved by any theory that is psychological in the strict sense. As we have repeatedly highlighted, Radical Behaviorism does not explicitly admits the explanatory validity of (2) subjective variables. Thus, Radical Behaviorism seeks for an intent in Evolutionary Psychology that explains and gives meaning to behavior emitted for the first time and seeks for an intent in the history of positive and negative consequences that explains exactly and gives meaning to a behavior already endowed with a history.

The (4) consequences of (3) behavior only reinforce or extinguish behavior because (3) it has its own (2) intent. (3) Behavior can have a (4) consequence that is different from its (2) original intent, and this (4) consequence may reveal itself more (2) satisfactory or (2) satisfactory in a different sense than the sense originally sought. The child who (3) cries to (2) quench his/her hunger may receive, in addition to (2) the satisfaction pursued, a different type of (2) satisfaction: the attention of his/her parents. Parental attention is a (4) consequence derived from (3) crying that was not phylogenetically programmed. But, that does not allow us to say that the parents' attention, as a (4) consequence of (3) crying, becomes its (2) intent. We only speak of (4) parental attention as (2) the intent of (3) crying because we wrongly identify the (2) satisfaction found in the (4) attention with the (4) attention itself. Fallacious theories such as Radical Behaviorism and language mistakes produce lapses in the way we think. In trying to find a behavioral sense that replaces the psychological sense of behavior and makes it superfluous, Radical Behaviorism confuses consequence with intent.

Consequence is not intent. Darwin was quite clear on this point: evolutionary reasons are not finalists. Evolutionary reasons show positive consequences of an organ or behavior which, because of its adaptive value, allowed its selection and its genetic transmission to subsequent generations. However, each selected organ or behavior already had its own intent from the beginning; this intent is what gives us the meaning of its activity or emission; this intent is its only explanatory reason.

Therefore, the theory of evolution does not explain the intent of an organ or behavior. It does not explain, for instance, the intent of a bird's wings. The intent of a bird's wings is flying! The theory of evolution explains how the positive consequences of the flight of birds might represent an advantage over other non-winged species which made possible the reproduction of birds that are capable of flying and the transmission of this ability to future generations. Evolutionary Psychology does not explain the act of crying. The intent of crying is to ask for help in satiating hunger! Evolutionary Psychology speculates on the positive consequences of crying and claims that they represented an advantage so that human reproduction and the transmission of the crying capacity to babies of future generations became possible over other species whose babies did not cry. Similarly, (4) parental attention does not explain the (3) individual cry of any baby. The intent of a (3) baby's cry, the crying of any baby in the world, will always be to ask for help in finding (2) satiety. It is the pursuit of (2) satiety which explains and gives meaning to (3) crying. The (4) parental attention history only explains how (3) the act of crying, having found in (4) parental attention a (2) different satisfaction from the (2) satisfaction it phylogenetically sought, increased its emission frequency, being later emitted even when the child was not (2) hungry and was grown up and able to (3) to feed him/herself.

In the same way evolutionary reasons show only the conditions that made the genetic transmission of an organ or behavior possible without elucidating the intent that really explains it, behavior analysis shows only the (4) consequences which increase or decrease the emission frequency of a certain (3) behavior and does not clarify the (2) intent that actually explains it. The (2) intent of a (3) behavior may be phylogenetic and refer to the evolutionary history of a species or it may be learned and refer to the (4) history of its consequences in each individual. In both cases, the intent is neither elucidated by the analysis of phylogenetic evolution which points out the consequences of behavior for the species nor by analyzing the (3) behavior which points its (4) consequences in the individual case. Confusing intent with consequence, in both cases, is nothing but a mistake.

Skinner seems to agree with this conclusion:

> Early students of learning used mazes and other devices in which a goal seemed to show the position of a reinforcer with respect to the behavior of which it was a consequence; the organism went toward a goal. But the important relation is temporal, not spatial. Behavior is followed by reinforcement; it does not pursue and overtake it. (...) That is the only role of the future. Skinner, 1971, p. 142.

For Skinner, behavior is not teleological. It does not seek any intent. The relationship between (3) behavior and (4) reinforcement is mechanical and lifeless: (3) behavior is followed by (4) reinforcement, which increases the (3) behavior's frequency of emission. But the emission frequency of a (3) behavior does not mean it (2) will again seek the (4) consequence by which it was reinforced. (3) Behavior does not (2) seek the (4) reinforcement which has not yet been given; future events are not the cause of behavior; the effect cannot temporally precede its cause; (4) reinforcement inasmuch as the cause of a (3) behavior, must precede it. If Skinner were to admit that (3) behavior "seeks" something, he would be giving way to the "autonomous man" paradigm and admitting that the individual's private and inaccessible interior is, somehow, source to the start of a (3) behavior. But according to the internalism critics, (3) behavior cannot start in the (2) man's interior; (3) behavior is a function of (1) (4) environmental contingencies; it is controlled by the environment.

However, the undeniable truth appears thereupon:

> The primate hand evolved in order that things might be more successfully manipulated, but its purpose is to be found not in a prior design but rather in the process of selection. Similarly, in operant conditioning the purpose of a skilled movement of the hand is to be found in the consequences which follow it. Skinner, 1971, p. 204

Skinner struggled to hide the (2) mentalist sense of (3) behavior in scientific rationalizations that specialized in speaking of behavior without making direct reference to it. The whole aim of his rationalizations was to replace the concept of (2) subjective control by the (1) (4) environment control. Evidently, in order for (1) (4) the environment control to replace (2) subjective control, the two types of control should perform the same function… and the function of (2) subjective control is to provide an intent to the (3) behavior being explained. It was therefore inevitable that the (1) (4) environment control had to perform the same function. And in the impossibility to translate the "intent" sense in a functional equation between (3) behavior and (1) (4) environmental contingencies, Skinner sees himself forced to use the mentalist expression "purpose", surreptitiously acknowledging the impossibility of reducing the (2) subjective sense of (3) behavior to functional relationships with (1) (4) environmental contingencies.

6 - Elucidating the Distinction between the "World outside the Skin" and the "World within the Skin"

The purpose of Evolutionary Psychology remains unclear. If what matters to Evolutionary Psychology is studying the adaptive function of behavior or the adaptive function of Darwinian algorithms, it would be enough to study their current adaptive function - if it really exists. What is the theoretical relevance of researches on the mind's evolutionary history? It seems that the sole purpose of Evolutionary Psychology is to provide Psychology with a scientific sense. Evolutionist psychologists take advantage of the scientific reputation of the evolution theory - according to Popper's negativity, the theory of evolution is not even a scientific discipline - and elaborate a psychological theory in the same way to thereby give - through "osmosis" - Psychology a scientific character that it never managed to acquire by its own merits.

However, if Evolutionary Psychology is theoretically irrelevant, this only occurs because it is also irrelevant in practice. Pragmatically, if we define a psychological theory, we can say that "psychological theories" are those which have some use for psychology practice in any of its areas or functions. Thus, in principle, biological theories are excluded from the list of psychological theories. For example, which professional psychology practice can be based on biological knowledge of the neural processes involved in depression? In turn, knowledge of the emotional processes involved in depression may be the basis of a psychologist's intervention in the case of a depressed client. At first, in order for biological theories to serve as basis for psychological interventions, the translation of the biological language into psychological language would be necessary. But this is not possible. Likewise, how could the behavior analyst make useful the theory which says that the adaptive function of the sexual act is reproduction, the adaptive function of jealousy is to ensure the gene transmission of one male to the detriment of another or the adaptive function of fear is the individual preservation? What kind of clinical intervention could be based on that knowledge in the treatment of a twenty-first century male sex addict who suffers from obsessive jealousy and is tormented with death thoughts? Would we treat his addiction to sex by appealing to the theory that, as a male of the human species, he is phylogenetically programmed to have sex for as many times and with as many partners he can? Would we treat his obsessive jealousy by appealing to the theory that, as male of the human species, he is phylogenetically programmed to trying to keep sexual exclusivity with as many women as he can? What about the death thoughts that torment him? Will we treat these thoughts by appealing to the theory that, as an individual of the human species, he is phylogenetically programmed to avoid death itself, for the benefit of his kind?

What insights can we expect the client to have from this type of intervention? What changes in the (1) initial conditions of (3) behavior or in its (4) reinforcement contingencies can a behavior analyst thus promote? The practical irrelevance of such theory is absolute. Its theoretical and practical value is null. Any psychological theory, however simple, has infinite practical value if compared to evolutionary theories. Because any value, as small as it might be, is infinitely greater than zero. If instead of the evolutionary theories mentioned above - or any other theory, it does not matter – we were to associate the pleasure of intercourse to the compensation for frustrated fulfillment in other forms of human relationships, the sex addiction problem would be attacked far more clearly and much more significant interventions could be promoted. If we related the possessiveness addressed to the sexual partner to the client's lack of him/herself, significant interventions could also be promoted. And if the meaning of "death" was analyzed and understood as the deprivation of the relationship with objects that constitute the subject's identity, a mature intervention would be possible in the case of the death thoughts that disturb the client. These are just examples of psychological theories that could be used. Any other theory, as simple or absurd as they may seem to some, would be infinitely more valuable than evolutionary theories, provided they were purely psychological.

Psychological theories are mentalist, and Radical Behaviorism proposed to abolish the mentalism from its theoretical system. However, when seeking for the meaning of behavior in evolutionism instead of mentalism, Radical Behaviorism contradicted one of its most cherished principles, pragmatism. The controversial simplicity of behavioral theories in comparison with psychological theories and the emphasis on environmental causes of behavior obey the principle that says practical results are more important than pretty and unnecessary theories. Skinner's intention was to present the scientific world with a behavior analysis methodology that was efficient for both experimental control and psychological interventions. However, psychological theories, even though accused by Skinner of being speculative and pseudo-explanatory, are still much more useful in experimental behavior control and in therapeutic behavioral interventions than evolutionary theories, since the practical value of the latter is null. So what would motivate Skinner to give up mentalism in favor of evolutionism?

The reason that made Radical Behaviorism opt for evolutionism is the same that guided the Evolutionary Psychology: the search for the scientific character. When the value attributed to scientific theories becomes so high as to motivate researchers to distinguish the theories with which they interact as "scientific" and "nonscientific", attributing all validity to the former at the expense of the latter, regardless of the value both have proved to have in practice, then that epistemological principle known as *scientism* is clearly characterized.

It does not matter if a given theory is scientific and has practical application in another discipline. In order for it to be a valid psychological theory, it must prove its value in the psychologist's practice care. Adopting scientific theories - valid in other fields and without any practical value for Psychology - over non-scientific theories that are valuable for psychological practice is scientistic conduct: Science is always the most important, even when it carries no significance.

There are two ways to judge the validity of a theory. One of them is adopted by scientism. *A priori*, the scientistic conduct considers as a valid assumption that only scientific theories are reliable and acceptable. In this sense, scientistics distinguishes theories as "scientific" and "non-scientific" and judge their validity by such discrimination. The scientistic paradigm functions, then, as a criterion for external validity. They do not judge a theory by analyzing its premises. It is judged by the sieve of premises that belong to a different theory, scientism, and validated according to how it fits them or not. Metaphorically speaking, it is like the theory rejected by scientism was a house knocked down from the outside, by the force of a crane. The second way to judge the validity of a theory is to refute it from its weaknesses. It is as if, instead of bringing down the house with a crane, we entered it, investigated it to its structural flaws so that, by exploring them, we would cause it to collapse under its own contingencies. This is the only honest and acceptable way to judge the validity of a theory, and that is exactly why it is the least used method.

Scientism's way of judging was also used by Skinner in the case of internalism. Skinner founded the philosophy of internalism supported by a language addiction. Indeed, our language allows us to talk about an action without explicitly mentioning the subjective intent that caused it. That is why, for instance, the statement "the mouse (3) ate because it was (1) deprived of food" seems intelligible even though the subjective intention - (2) the desire to satisfy hunger - is implicit and not directly mentioned. But our language also allows us to speak of (2) desires, beliefs and intentions alone without mentioning directly the (1) object to which they refer. Every desire is a desire for someone, something or some condition. People, things, and conditions are the objects of desire, and are environmental contingencies. Wanting is a way to relate; desire is a form of relationship and every relationship occurs between subject and object. However, the habit of talking about desire not mentioning its object resulted in giving the object the status of a "thing". We spoke about desire for so long without mentioning its object, without even stopping to think what its object really is, that we finally ended up speaking of it as an existing thing *per se*; something that exists independently of both subject and object, of which it is an affective relationship. And when the relationship between subject and object becomes a thing, it becomes an object. But it is not just any object. It is a missing object in the world of objects. Indeed, this "object-desire" is not among people, things and conditions. It is not an environmental contingency; therefore, it can neither be found in the physical nor in the cultural environment. The world of objects is the physical and cultural environment; the physical and cultural environment is the objective world. Absent from the objective world, desire is restricted to the subjective world; and the subjective world, since absent from the physical and cultural environment that exists "outside the skin", is forced to establish its existence in the world "within the skin", the individual's private world, inaccessible to the rest of the people.

It was thus bewitched, deceived and fooled by our language artifices that Skinner invented the distinction between "world within the skin" and "world outside the skin". Our language played tricks on him and he fell for it. From that point on, he defined internalism and established as a valid *a priori* assumption the inadequacy of explanations based on all psychological theory from which it was possible to identify assumptions compatible with the definition previously provided by it. Internalism became the decisive sieve for evaluating a psychological theory's validity or unsuitability to Skinner's Radical Behaviorism. And since all psychological theories except for Radical Behaviorism could be accused of being internalist in the author's point of view, he felt entitled to refuse them all at once and to elect Radical Behaviorism as the only valid psychology.

Skinner advocates the existence of two worlds distinguished by the access road: the world outside the skin is accessible to the public; the world within the skin is private. Only the individual has access to his world within the skin. According to this view, the subjective world is interior and inaccessible to the public while the objective world is outside and accessible. However, desire, fear, beliefs and all other categories of the "subjective world" represent relations with objects in the world outside the skin; they are, in this sense, related to the object or objective. They can be described both by Radical Behaviorism's objective vocabulary, which leaves implicit all references to (2) subjectivity, and by the subjective vocabulary of psychological theories, which can leave implicit all references to (1) environmental contingencies.

The difference between a psychological explanation and a behavior analysis is merely linguistic. Both deal with the same relationship between subject and object, both fall within the same world. However, psychological explanations are subjective, that is, their language is subjective. Behavior analyses, on the other hand, are objective and their language is objective. There are not two worlds, one outside the skin and another within the skin. There is only one world, the world in which the behavior takes place, and the behavior can be described by both subjective and objective language.

It is possible that behavior analysts and scientists in general agree that the difference between a psychological explanation and a behavior analysis is a linguistic one. However, they would agree on that point to immediately return to the accessibility issue: Even though the difference is language, describing behavior in subjective language requires the inference of internal states accessible only to the individual, while the description in objective language is restricted to publicly accessible environmental conditions.

I could respond by saying that: a) objective explanations are also inferential, since it is not possible to know and control all variables at play in a natural system, and that b) behavior analyses do not circumvent and do not exclude inferences about private subjective states by describing behavior alone without making direct reference to them. However, at this point we need to acknowledge the behaviorists and scientists are correct. What compels me say they are right is precisely the language issue. For the language we have at our disposal to describe the (1) environmental contingencies of (3) behavior is much more accurate than the language used to describe (2) subjective states. The vagueness of subjective language means uncertainty: Are we properly speaking about what other people (2) think and feel when we describe subjective states? The accuracy of objective language means certainty: When describing (1) environmental contingencies, we are properly talking about what people other than us can experience by means of the five classic senses (sight, hearing, touch, smell and taste). The uncertainty which lies immanent to the descriptions of (2) subjective states refers to the notion of inference: We are not sure what other people are (2) thinking or feeling, we are only inferring that they think and feel the way described. The certainty immanent to descriptions of (1) environmental contingencies refers to the notion of direct and universal access: We are sure that, in describing (1) environmental contingencies, we are talking about what is really there.

The difference in accuracy between the subjective and the objective language certainly offers a justification for the theoretical division between a world outside the skin and the other world within the skin. However, the misconception of this division lies in the confusion that takes the imprecision of subjective language as a reflection of the vagueness and obscurity of subjectivity: The subjective world is inherently imprecise, unclear and therefore accessible only by inferences that are groping in the dark. However, the vagueness and obscurity of the subjective world are not ontological; they are not properties of its "nature". The vagueness and obscurity of the subjective world are contingencies of our culture.

Small children experience a range of sensorial and affective experiences, both perceptual and imaginative. They neither have the necessary language to express them nor to distinguish real from fanciful, subjective from objective experiences. In conversations with adults, children acquire accurate signs to designate the objects in the world outside the skin. Consequently, they learn to express themselves about the reality of the objective world with increasing accuracy. Reports and statements judged by others as "fanciful" are corrected and replaced by descriptions considered compatible with the adult paradigm of "reality".

As children's reports and assertions about the objective world are validated and verified by adults, they begin to feel safe to classify the world outside the skin as "reality" without needing confirmation from anyone. They become independent from other people's confirmation as the history of previous conversations allows them to extract the paradigm of what will be approved by the adults and what will be rejected. The reality paradigm that children begin to draw from their life experience has only one meaning: That which is part of general consent is real, and that which is generally rejected is unreal. "Reality" is nothing more than the set of premises and assertions of general consent.

The reality paradigm provides the child with the criterion that precisely distinguishes what is real from what is unreal. The "unreal" contains both assumptions and assertions defined as "imaginary" and those which mistakenly describe the objective world. The child who wakes up at night afraid of the monster under the bed will be corrected by the adult who will try to convince the child that the monster exists only in his/her imagination, and that there are no such things in the real world.

And the child who confronts an adult with the theory that the sun hides behind the mountain at dusk will be corrected (hopefully) with the correct description of this objective fact.

But the reality paradigm does not distinguish only the real from the unreal; it also distinguishes the objective from the subjective. The subjective world is not necessarily unrealistic; the imaginary world, which creates monsters under the bed, it is certainly defined as unreal. Overall, the subjective world is not unreal. While the objective reality becomes universal and has collective assent, the subjective reality remains private and related only to the individual. This difference is explained by the habit of talking about objective reality. We are introduced to the habit of talking about it in our early years. Consequently, besides the improvement of a precise vocabulary to refer to (1) environmental contingencies of the "world outside the skin" done by our culture, each of us develops, in the first years of life, the belief that the most basic assertions and reports about the objective world have everyone's approval. The subjective world is not unreal. We just don't create the habit of talking about it. Hence, a precise vocabulary to refer to (2) subjective states of the "world within the skin" has not been improved by our culture, and so each of us develops, from the early childhood years up to adulthood, the belief that the most basic assertions and accounts of the subjective world relate only to our private reality, they are only true for ourselves and not for others, and there is no possibility of general assent for any fact from this obscure world.

In the absence of the habit of talking about the subjective world, one develops the belief that there are, in fact, many subjective worlds and there are as many subjective worlds as there are people. According to this belief, each person has their own private subjective world, and what happens in someone's subjective world is inaccessible to the subjective world of others. However, cultivating the habit of talking about thoughts and feelings would certainly force the development of a more precise vocabulary, and as reports and statements about (2) subjective states receive more and more collective approval, the belief that they are universal and open to collective inspection would gain more weight.

However, scientistics and behaviorists would object, this theory overrides the facts. It is true that (2) the individual's subjective states are private and no one can know them unless the individual talks about them. And even if he expresses them, we will never be sure if he/she is being sincere or not. And even if he/she is being honest, we will never be sure if his sincerity is true to the facts. As to the description of (1) environmental contingencies, these questions do not persist. One does not need to communicate the intuition of an objective fact that occurs in an open, free access environment to make sure that it can be perceived and known by all. And when an objective intuition is verbalized, we are immediately sure of its correctness from the comparison with the report that we ourselves would make about it.

What serves as basis for the certainty that an objective fact occurring in open, free access environment can be shared by all present? This certainty is based on the habit. From our experience we have learned that basic assertions and reports about the objective world receive collective approval. Yet we cannot know the contents of any intuition beyond our own. Even if a friend, at our request, verbalizes the contents of his present objective intuition, we will not be allowed to conclude that he is telling the truth. And we still won't be allowed to conclude that he is telling the truth even if his account matches our own account of the same facts. Therefore, we are also not allowed to conclude that he is lying if his account differs from ours. Science itself has already testified that each individual's objective intuition is relatively different. Thus, the difference in reports does not necessarily mean that some are right and others are wrong, let alone that there are liars among the reporters. Also, the similarity of the reports does not allow us to conclude that the same intuition is shared by all or that all reporters are telling the truth. Indeed, although the assumptions and assertions of different accounts of the same objective fact coincide, the meaning given to them by each reporter still won't be the same. We all learn to use the same words to describe each (1) environmental contingency; we learn which word, statement or report receives collective approval when used in the description of a given (1) environmental contingency. But that does not allow us to conclude that our intuition of an objective fact occurred in open, free access environment is shared by all present. We will never know the true contents of an intuition that is different from our own. Therefore, the assumption that objective facts occurred in open, free access environments can be shared by all who are present, is nothing but an inference.

In talking about the objective world, only the most basic reports and assertions receive collective approval. The more detailed the analysis and the more profuse the relations between one (1) contingency and (1) another, the more and more subject to disagreement with the current opinion the reports and statements about the objective world become; thus, the more "subjective" they become. "Subjective", according to our cultural reality paradigm, is every private, subject-related reality that is not necessarily wrong, but has no assurance of collective approval. That is why the ideal of objectivity is intertwined with simplicity: objective descriptions are as simple as possible. Any addition to simplicity may already imply subjectivity.

In talking about the subjective world, even the most basic reports and assertions do not receive collective approval. That is why even the most basic concepts and definitions of subjective language are subject to controversy. In the absence of collective approval for even the simplest subjective facts, the fact that the correlation between what a third person thinks and feels and what we intuit about his thoughts and feelings is merely inferential or doubtful becomes clear. Had we cultivated the habit of talking about (2) subjective states until the psychological language had achieved the accuracy needed to produce the collective approval of statements and reports relating to its simplest subjective facts, we would also believe that the intuition of these facts is open to public share, even though we never lost consciousness that it is possible to hide from others what we really feel and think. The belief in the public share of our subjectivity is not based on the possibility of having others feel what we feel or think what we think. It is based, instead, on the certainty that the communication of statements and reports on elementary subjective facts would be received with collective approval, as occurs with the belief on public sharing objective intuitions. This certainty is what underlies the belief - or illusion - that intuition of elementary objective facts occurred in open, free access spaces is universal - even though we continue believing it is possible to hide from others what we are really seeing, hearing, etc. The same certainty would also justify the belief that the elementary facts of our (2) feelings and thoughts are universal and shared by all, or the illusion that everyone thinks and feels basically like we think and feel ourselves.

The belief that all think and feel basically like we feel and think does not contradict the belief that it is possible to hide what we really feel and think. The belief of universally sharing elementary facts of the subjective world would be founded solely in the habit of receiving collective approval - granted to statements and reports of elementary subjective facts - made possible by the precision of the subjective language. But the precise language of subjective reports and statements about elementary subjective facts would still end the possibility of giving them senses that are individual and inaccessible to others. Not to mention reports and statements on complex subjective facts. In those cases, the weight of individuality is even greater, the possibility of divergence with the current opinion too, and the belief in the possibility of universal sharing is therefore much lower.

The great objection to this hypothesis is: How is it possible to believe that, for instance, all the people with us around a bar table are basically thinking and feeling the same way we think and feel just as we believe that they all see the same beer bottles on the table and listen to the same music? Certainly, it is possible that each of these people is in a different state of mind and have completely different thoughts from those of the rest. Believing that we think and feel the same way as our friends is possible. However, it is very rare and means that deep, satisfying sense of intimacy. In any case, this is not the belief we are dealing with. We are not referring to the belief that we are feeling and thinking, in real time, the same as so many other people. Our object of study is the behavior. Behaviorists argue that the objective description of (1) environmental contingencies and (4) reinforcements present the (3) behavior in a universal form shareable by all. Nonetheless, since the meaning of behavioral analyses is (2) subjective, this meaning must also be universally shareable by all. If the objective description of behavior is universal and open to the public, its meaning is also; and if this meaning is subjective, then the (2) subjective states which give it meaning are universal and accessible to the public, rather than private and inaccessible to others. In short, we are dealing with the following assumption: If subjective language were as refined as objective language, we would be accustomed to believe that the (2) subjective nature of any person's (3) behavior is as evident, universal, and open to public inspection as its objective nature.

That is not what behaviorists claim. The entire theoretical foundation of Radical Behaviorism is the claim that (1) environmental contingencies and contingencies that (4) reinforce (3) behavior are objective and publicly accessible, while its (2) subjective states are private and accessible only to the individual. The foundation of such mistaken belief is the embryonic state of our subjective language. Although it is possible to give a precise and universal description to (1) environmental and (4) reinforcement contingencies of (3) behavior, its (2) subjective, though equally universal sense, reveals itself controversial when we strive to verbalize it and describe it in the appropriate subjective conceptual terms. It is safer, therefore, to keep them implicit and unspoken. We understand better about our (2) subjective states when we leave them implicit than when we try to talk about them. Hence the conclusion that each person's (2) subjective world is private and accessible only to the individual.

If the subjective language suffered improvements and became accurate enough to produce in us the certainty that our reports and assertions about elementary subjective facts would receive collective approval, we would believe from our early years that we basically think and feel the same way as others. In practice, this belief would mean that the (2) elementary subjective sense of our (3) behavior would be universal and accessible to all, once anyone could describe it in appropriate subjective language without any controversy. Believing in the universal and accurate access to our (2) subjective states would make subjectivity as objective as (1) environmental and (4) reinforcement contingencies of (3) behavior are believed to be.

The objectivity of subjectivity does not depend on the possibility of directly accessing people's "within", private world. Universal access to (1) environmental and (4) reinforcement contingencies of (3) behavior is a belief; as such, according to the very definition of Radical Behaviorism, it is a (3) behavior to be explained by analyzing its own (1) (4) contingencies. The contingencies that (4) reinforce (3) the belief in universal access to (1) (4) contingencies of (3) individual behavior are the collective approvals to reports and claims about elementary objective facts. But, strictly speaking, the belief in the universal accessibility of (3) behavior (1) (4) contingencies is as inferential as we now believe to be our knowledge of (2) subjective states. Consequently, if we had (4) reinforced our ability to (3) talk about subjective states in the same way we (4) reinforced our ability to (3) talk about environmental and reinforcement contingencies, the belief in the universal access to our (2) elementary subjective states would be as strong as is now our belief in the universal access of (1) (4) the contingencies of (3) individual behavior.

In order for subjectivity to become objective, we don't need to have direct access to the thoughts and feelings of anyone; we must only learn to speak properly about our (2) subjective states. There is no such thing as two worlds - an objective and a subjective world. There is only one world that can be described by objective or subjective language. If (3) behavior can be treated objectively, the (2) subjectivity which gives it meaning can also be treated objectively. And, contrary to what is commonly thought, the objective treatment of (2) subjectivity does not mean to describe it in objective language. It is precisely the use of appropriate subjective language that can provide (2) subjectivity with the objectivity it has never had thus far.

The illusion of a world divided in "within the skin" and "outside the skin" can be explained by the contingency of our culture not having sufficiently developed its subjective language to objectively treat (2) subjectivity. This contingency explains but does not justify the philosophy of Skinner's internalism. For even though it is grounded in the contingencies of our culture, this philosophy is nonetheless extremely naïve and greatly ineffective as criticism. It is the duty of every thinker to try and go beyond the ordinary limits of his/her culture. Rather than throwing Psychology beyond its own time, Skinner sank to the limited paradigms of his time.

The illusory division of a world "within the skin" that is private and inaccessible to the public and a world "outside the skin" that is universal and freely accessible can be explained by the contingencies of our culture, the assumption that all psychologies which seek (2) subjective explanations disregard or lose focus of (1) environmental contingencies cannot be explained, let alone justified by cultural contingency. All we have got to do is open our eyes and enhance our senses to realize that every (2) desire, fear, or belief has as its object an (1) environmental contingency and that one thing is already implicit when we speak of another. The belief that the focus on (2) subjectivity obscures and prevents the analysis of (1) environmental contingencies is simply unrealistic. And if this fantasy has the power to convince so many people, they prefer to see the world through the eyes of others than to open and see with their own.

The secret of objective psychology is not the discovery of a specific experimentation method, much less a way of entering what others think and feel. The subjective speaking which makes subjectivity objective is the basis of the objective psychology we are all looking for. More than that, it is the cure for the loneliness of those who believe they think and feel differently from what others think and feel.

7 - The Empty Sense of Behavior Analysis and the Way to True Objective Psychology

The philosophy of internalism preaches the existence of two worlds separated in regards to their "accessibility": The world within the skin and the world outside the skin. The world within the skin is private and accessible only to the individual; the world outside the skin is universal and accessible to all. Skinner's critique of internalism can be summarized as follows: If (3) behavior is a function of (2) internal variables, you cannot modify it. (2) Internal variables are inaccessible to others and therefore one cannot directly interfere in them. However, if (2) internal variables are a function of (1) (4) external variables as well as the (3) behavior, this means if we alter the (1) (4) external variables of which they are a function, we will also be modifying (3) behavior itself. It is a fact that (3) behavior can be modified. And if it can be modified, then it is a function of (1) (4) external variables, once the exclusive relationship with (2) internal variables would make it inaccessible to any intervention. Consequently, the study of (3) behavior must focus on the analysis of (1) (4) external variables. The focus on (2) internal variables is unproductive for two reasons: In addition to not revealing any changeable contingency, it withdraws the attention of (1) (4) environmental contingencies of which (3) behavior is a function. This assumption justifies the claim that behavior analysis cannot contain mentalist expressions. Mentalist expressions refer to (2) internal variables. Therefore, every time a mentalist expression appears in behavior analysis, this can only mean that important (1) (4) environmental contingencies in the explanation are being ignored.

Skinner's thesis is logical, but it does not correspond to the facts. For this reason, when the author uses examples to justify his thesis, they openly reveal his fraud:

> The mental explanation brings curiosity to an end. We see the effect in casual discourse. If we ask someone, "Why did you go to the theater?" and he says, "Because I felt like going," we are apt to take his reply as a kind of explanation. It would be much more the point to know what has happened when he has gone to the theater in the past, what he heard or read about the play he went to see, and what other things in his past or present environments might have induced him to go (as opposed to doing something else), but we accept "I felt

like going" as a sort of summary of all this and are not likely to ask for details. Skinner, 1971, pp. 12-13.

In our society, who in good conscience would accept the answer "Because I felt like going" as a satisfactory response or sufficient reason, say, to go to the theater, or to take any other action? It is so unsatisfactory that we consider it rude or impolite. Anyone who receives such response will be inclined to ask for more details or a truly explanatory reason. If they don't, it will be due to specific contingencies of the relationship with their interlocutor or other circumstantial reasons.

This type of response is unsatisfactory because the (2) will to go to the theater is implicit in the (3) action of going to the theater. In answering "we (3) went to the theater because (2) we felt like going", we are informing our interlocutor something he/she already knew and we knew that he/she knew, since (2) feeling like going, as a subjective sense of the (3) action of going to the theater by choice, is accessible to public observation. We are intentionally using as a response a variable that was already included in the question; we are not adding any explanatory variable to the response; therefore, we are not answering anything at all. This shows, contrary to what behaviorists argument, that the (2) subjective sense of (3) behavior is so public that it is obvious.

But if the (2) will to go to the theater does not provide a sufficient explanation or reason for the (3) action of going to the theater, this is due not to the fact that the explicit reference to the (2) will leaves in the dark the (1) (4) environmental contingencies that truly explain the (3) behavior. On the contrary, the (2) will does not explain anything precisely because we need the details so that (3) behavior becomes understandable. The (2) will needs to be analyzed. And the result of this analysis can be described in both (2) subjective and (1) (4) objective language.

The analysis is more commonly made in a speech that merges subjective and objective languages. This is our everyday language. The everyday language merges the subjective and objective vocabulary because the two types of vocabulary are implicit in each other. Every (2) desire, fear, or belief have an object, and that object is a (1) (4) world contingency. In turn, every (1) (4) world contingency, insofar as it is inserted into the subject's life history, is an object for its (2) desires, fears or beliefs. This relationship is so obvious that we learn to speak of (2) desires, fears, and beliefs without mentioning the (1) (4) contingencies attached to them. It is obvious because it is implicit and does not need explicit reference. Similarly, we learn to speak of the (1) (4) world contingencies without mentioning (2) desires, fears, and beliefs attached to them. It is obvious because it is implicit, and does not need explicit reference. When the reference to a person's (2) desires, fears, and beliefs does not provide a sufficient reason for his/her (3) behavior, this does not occur because the focus in (2) subjectivity removes the focus in (1) (4) world contingencies; this occurs because the relationship between the (2) subjective reason and the (3) behavior is too close or too obvious to be explanatory, making it necessary an amplitude increase that will make the reason sufficient. The (2) will go to the theater is as narrow a reason to explain the (3) action of going as the fact that (1) the play is being staged at the time. If so and so (3) goes to the theater for his own decision, it is obvious that he (2) feels like going to the theater and that (1) the play he likes is being staged at the time - or he believes the play is being staged. It is also obvious that he has had a (4) satisfying experience in the theater before, or he had experiences he judges similar to the experience of going to the theater, or he has – by other means – acknowledged experiences different from that of going to the theater that awoken his interest . None of these (1) (2) (4) reasons sufficiently explains behavior. And the reason why they do not explain anything is not at all related to their subjective or objective nature: They are too narrow or too allusive to be provided with sufficient explanatory value. Its amplitude must be increased. And this amplitude increase, consequently, does not need to be subjective or objective to provide (3) behavior with an explanation. The sufficiency or insufficiency of an explanation has nothing to do with its subjective or objective nature.

Subjectivity and objectivity are forms of language. Science is also a form of language. Subjective and objective languages do not exclude each other. When behavior is the object, these languages are implied in one another. Objectivity is not defined by public access and subjectivity is not defined by the characteristic isolation of private access. Subject and object are two universal and inseparable instances: A subject only exists if it is the subject of an object and an object only exists it is an object to a subject. The subject exists only in relation to the object and the object exists only in relation to the subject. Subjectivity and objectivity are two forms of language that describe the same relationship: While subjective language describes it in relation to the subject, objective language describes it in relation to the object. However, the subjective language that describes the relationship between subject and object brings implicit an objective sense, or a sense that is object-related; and the objective language that describes this relationship brings implicit a subjective sense, or a sense that is subject-related.

Behaviorists claim their language is objective. However, the sense of their analyses is subjective. The action of (3) going to the theater when (1) the play we expect is staged only becomes intelligible because (2) the will to go to the theater is implicit in the (3) action. Although, depending on the context, (2) the will to go to the theater may seem an insufficient explanation or reason for the action of (3) going, the meaning of the (3) action is given by the (2) will to go to the theater even when this meaning is not properly explained. Similarly, the (3) action of going to the theater when (2) we feel like it only becomes intelligible because the (2) will is related to an object, the (1) play being staged at the moment. The (2) will is always will of (3) doing something, and it is subject to (1) some present circumstance that is similar a number of previous circumstances in which the same (3) doing had (4) positive consequences.

It is impossible to speak of the (2) will to go to the theater without mentioning the (1) theatre and the circumstances surrounding it. But the will is connected to many objects. One can take something ordinary and universal from the relationship between the will and all its objects, which is the will itself. Clarifying the universal sense of the will helps us understand the meaning of the will in each of its particular relations. More than that: it helps us understand the meaning of the will in the specific (3) action of a particular subject, dated in time and space. The explanation of the universal sense of the will is a theory of the will; a psychological theory of the will. The will, studied in its universal sense, does not connect to any (1) particular condition or to any (3) particular action. Instead, it provides the general sense of will that helps clarify its specific meaning in each (3) particular action.

On the other hand, it is possible to speak of a (3) particularly action linked to the will to go to the theater, making no mention of (2) the will itself. We can explain the (3) action of going to the theater by mentioning only the (1) fact that the play we expected is being staged and the (4) nice consequences we experienced in past times when we (3) went to the theater. However, we cannot formulate any theory from the objective analysis of particular cases of the (3) action of going to the theater. A theory of (2) will is out of the question, since the will is not mentioned explicitly. And an objective and general theory of the (3) action of going to the theater is only possible in non-enlightening, allusive terms. In fact, an objective theory of (3) the action of going to the theater is no different from the objective theory of any other (3) behavior: The (3) action of going to the theater is explained by relating itself to its (1) initiating condition and the (4) history of its past consequences. But this is the behaviorist theory for any behavior! Any specification in the (1) initial conditions or in the (4) action consequences would transform the theory in the explanation of some particular case. Then, we would no longer be talking about a theory of the (3) action of going to the theater, we would be referring to the explanation of the (3) specific action of a particular subject, dated in time and space.

Even though the meaning of every behavior analysis is subjective, and that this meaning is only implicit in every analysis of this kind, the analysis of a (3) specific behavior, dated in time and space, may seem explanatory. However, the fraudulent nature of these explanations starkly reveals itself when behaviorists use their analysis to account for general cases and weave theories on behavior and society. Below is an example provided by Skinner himself, of the translation of psychological expressions into behavioral expressions:

> Consider a young man whose world has suddenly changed. He has graduated from college and is going to work, let us say, or has been inducted into the armed services. Most of the behavior he has acquired up to this point proves useless in his new environment. The behavior he actually exhibits can be described, and the description translated, as follows: he lacks assurance or feels insecure or is unsure of himself (*his behavior is weak and inappropriate*); he is dissatisfied or discouraged (*he is seldom reinforced, and as a result his behavior undergoes extinction*); he is frustrated (*extinction is accompanied by emotional responses*); he feels uneasy or anxious (*his behavior frequently has unavoidable aversive consequences which have emotional effects*); there is nothing he wants to do or enjoys doing well, he has no feeling of craftsmanship, no sense of leading a purposeful life, no sense of accomplishment (*he is rarely reinforced for doing anything*); he feels guilty or ashamed (*he has previously been punished for idleness or failure, which now evokes emotional responses*); he is disappointed in himself or disgusted with himself (*he is no longer reinforced by the admiration of others, and the extinction which follows has emotional effects*); he becomes hypochondriacal (*he concludes that he is ill*) or neurotic (*he engages in a variety of ineffective modes of escape*); and he experiences an identity crises (*he does not recognize the person he once called 'I'*). Skinner, 1971, pp. 146-147

Skinner does not address a general theory of behavior. He presents us the case of a specific behavior. But it is not the specific behavior, dated in time and space, of a particular subject. This is a behavior that can be observed in many young people who experience the condition he described. Still, he is unable to provide descriptions that are not vague and allusive. They seem intelligible, because their real sense, described in psychological terms, is given right after. But what would happen if we omitted the psychological expressions from the text? What kind of explanation would we be left with?

Let us see: *Consider a young man whose world has suddenly changed. He has graduated from college and is going to work, let us say, or has been inducted into the armed services. Most of the behavior he has acquired up to this point proves useless in his new environment. The behavior he actually exhibits can be described as follows: his behavior is weak and inappropriate; he is seldom reinforced, and as a result his behavior undergoes extinction; extinction is accompanied by emotional responses; his behavior frequently has unavoidable aversive consequences which have emotional effects; he is rarely reinforced for doing anything; he has previously been punished for idleness or failure, which now evokes emotional responses; he is no longer reinforced by the admiration of others, and the extinction which follows has emotional effects; he concludes that he is ill or he engages in a variety of ineffective modes of escape; he does not recognize the person he once called "I".*

If, instead of transcribing Skinner's original text I had firs transcribed the edited text above, would the reader know what Skinner was talking about? He couldn't have. And neither would an experienced behaviorist. How often does Skinner allude to "emotional effects" without really specifying anything about them? How often does he speak of "extinction" and "reinforcement" without saying what these concepts mean? He speaks of "negative consequences" without mentioning what these consequences really are. Which sane person could guess that "weak and inappropriate behavior" is the translation of "insecurity", for instance? And who could say that the conclusion of being ill is an obvious symptom of hypochondria?

In the excerpt above, Skinner made the translation of simple psychological expressions into behavioral expressions and still failed to provide anything but vague and allusive descriptions that do not convey the meaning that the author intended whatsoever. In fact, the reader is forced to guess the meaning of what Skinner is saying. It is not at all suitable for us to speak of "inference" here. There is no base for inferences. We need to guess the meaning of the author's words. And if the translation of simple psychological expressions into behavioral expressions produces nothing more than vague, allusive descriptions, what can we say about the attempts to use them for explaining human behavior in general? What can we say about its application in the explanation of social phenomena?

Behavior analysis only preserves its illusory intelligibility in describing the simple behavior of pigeons and rats in the apparatus that we have come to call "Skinner box". The expression "the mouse (3) ate because it was (1) deprived of food" seems intelligible. In fact, it is not intelligible by itself, but it seems to be. Applied in the explanation of general cases, of social phenomena, applied, finally, in real life, behavior analysis is nothing but a set of vague and allusive descriptions that explain nothing.

Subsequently to the excerpt transcribed (p. 147), Skinner says that the passages highlighted in italics are too brief to be accurate. However, the psychological expressions into which he intended to translate those passages are also the shortest possible. What can be briefer and more imprecise than "feels insecure"? And in any case, the meaning of the brief and inaccurate psychological expressions translated by him is much more specific and clear than the meaning of their behavioral translations. Skinner's criticism to the mentalist vocabulary is based precisely on the vagueness and on the little light shed on behavior by these subjective expressions. In addition, according to the author, subjective variables need to be inferred. But the effort to replace the mentalist vocabulary for an objective vocabulary produces only evasive, allusive, and vague explanations. The greater the complexity of the behavior or social phenomenon studied, the more evasive, elusive, and vague is its behavioral explanation and the more inferential is its meaning.

Behavioral explanations are vague, allusive, and elusive because they do not approach what's essential. Skinner taught us to speak - or to try to speak - about the essential without putting it into words. Such questionable art he improved while searching for behavioral translations for mentalist expressions. It is the author himself who speaks of translations, as in the quoted passage. The behaviorist thinks in mentalist terms, but speaks in behavioral terms; he/she seeks to express in behavioral language the mentalist sense in which he thinks but cannot verbalize. Consequently, he/she produces nothing but allusive, evasive, and vague metaphors; objectively-disguised metaphors which hide - or strive to hide – their subjective, mentalist, or psychological meaning. In psychology, the essential is subjective, not objective. Psychology, in its strictest sense, is the science of subjectivity.

In fact, a science of subjectivity is that Psychology should be, not what it is today. In order for this science to fulfill its role, it must present subjectivity in its universal laws. Universality and access to public verification is what is understood for "objectivity". Thus, for Psychology to become the science of subjectivity, it must present subjectivity in an objective way.

This objectivity whose meaning is intertwined with the meaning of universality and possibility of public verification does not need to be forged and artificially attributed to Psychology. Subjectivity is objective in nature. Behavioral explanations prove that to us. According to Radical Behaviorism, if behavior can be explained by universal laws and in a publicly accessible way and the meaning of these explanations is subjective, then this subjectivity, in addition to having its universal laws, is also verifiable. If the explanation for the mouse's (3) act of eating is associated to (1) food deprivation, and if this association follows objective behavioral laws which can be publicly verified, then its meaning also follows universal laws that can also be publicly verified. The mouse's (2) hunger is what gives meaning to this explanation; it only makes sense because the association of (2) hunger, (1) food deprivation and the (3) act of eating is as necessary, universal, and verifiable publicly as any objective law. However, if we try to translate into subjective expressions the laws which govern (2) hunger, we will probably disagree. These laws are known intuitively. We observe them in their objective aspect in the behavior of animals and humans, but if we try to put them in the appropriate subjective terms, we will generate more confusion than clarification.

The confusion would be generated for two reasons: First, our culture hasn't improved subjective language as precisely as it improved objective language. Consequently, the meaning of our subjective expressions is still ambiguous and imprecise. Second, it is very likely that, in trying to explain hunger in its subjective universal laws, we would make use of specific environmental conditions, such as (1) food deprivation. And when we condition a subjective theory to a specific condition instead of portraying subjectivity in its universal laws, we explain specific cases of behavior emitted under specific conditions. Subjectivity, portrayed in its universal laws, does not relate to specific conditions; its laws are valid for all conditions. This is the meaning of a general law.

Subjectivity is not disconnected from the world. Differently from Skinner's accusation, Psychology does not ignore the environment when analyzing (2) subjective motivations. But even physical sciences do not elaborate their laws in relation to (1) specific environmental conditions. The formula $f = m.a$ does not relate to any (1) specific condition. It is a general law, and therefore valid for all conditions. Subjective language describes the relationship between subject and object from a subjective point of view. In order for the subjectivity thus described to become universal, it cannot be connected to any (1) specific condition. It should speak of the relationship between subject and object only in subjective terms, without specifying any (1) environmental condition.

We are not trained to do so. We are so used to understanding the subjectivity implicit in (3) behavior linked to (1) specific conditions that we do not know how to speak about it in any other way. When trying to verbalize it in universal format, we treat it in relation to some (3) specific behavior that occurs or occurred in a (1) given situation. And so we disagree to the extent that each of us wants to explain subjectivity relating it to a (3) chosen specific behavior and to a (1) specific condition of our choice. Consequently, we nurture the belief that subjectivity does not have a universal form, that subjective laws that apply to one do not apply to others and, therefore, that our understanding of other people's subjectivity is merely inferential and speculative. Skinner did not push Psychology ahead a single step. He only sank it further in the wrong prejudices with which it always struggled in common sense.

Only a completely subjective Psychology can portray subjectivity in its general laws. However, it does not suffice that it is completely subjective. The universal and publicly verifiable subjectivity is that which is implicit in the behavior. And every behavior has a purpose; every behavior has an object; every behavior has an objective; every behavior is objective. Every behavior is objective because it is linked to an object; that is its objectivity. If subjectivity is what gives meaning to behavior, then it is impossible to disentangle subjectivity from objective behavior. The subjectivity of behavior is identical to its objectivity. Its subjectivity refers to the subject who behaves, its objectivity refers to the object with which the subject relates; therefore, in the sphere of behavior, subject and object are identical.

The subjectivism which is lost from the identity with the object wanders aimlessly and gives reason to criticism from those who have always depreciated the subjective thinking. Psychology is only objective when it considers the identity between subject and object. However, subject and object are clearly different. In the sphere of behavior, the objective is that which has not been realized; it is the intent that has not been met by behavior. The objective of behavior is to perform its relation with the object; this is its subjective sense. The meaning of behavior is only fulfilled when the behavior comes to an end; but when does the behavior end? We never stop acting. If the meaning of behavior is only achieved with the fulfillment of its purpose, and that purpose is never achieved, then its meaning never takes place. Furthermore: If the unrealized sense of behavior is its subjectivity, and if its subjectivity is related to the acting subject, then the acting subject remains unfulfilled as such. The subject's realization would coincide with his/her objective achievement; but the objectively fulfilled subject becomes the object, or rather, he would become identical to his/her object. The subject's nature is to be identical to the object; however, since it is not realized in action, subject and object remain distinct.

The distinction between subject and object occurs in the field of their identity; hence they remain related. Subject and object connect through identity. Their identity is what keeps them related through the difference that lies between them. The difference exists in the identity and the identity exists in the difference. Difference never rests; it reproduces at all times in the identity that keeps undoing it. Identity never rests; it reproduces at all times in the difference that never ceases to undo it. The relationship between subject and object is always moving; it is a *dynamic* relationship.

What is objective Psychology? It is the psychology that portrays the dynamics of identity and difference between subject and object from the subjective point of view. To fulfill its role, objective Psychology must be completely subjective. It must thoroughly explain subjectivity for itself. In that sense, it seeks behavior's deepest subjective roots, and therefore deserves to be named *Radical Mentalism*. Objective Psychology is the reconciliation of Psychology with its own language.

CONCLUSION

Behavior analysis is unintelligible, inferential, inaccurate and non-explanatory. The only variable that gives it meaning is the (2) subjective variable, which Skinner's critical philosophy to internalism intended to eliminate. When it is impossible for one to infer the (2) subjective sense in a behavior analysis, there is nothing that can save its intelligibility façade. In turn, compared to behavior analysis, psychological or mentalist explanations are accurate, intelligible, objective and non-inferential.

This is the synthesized conclusion of my brief study. Evidently, these are conclusions based on Radical Behaviorism as a critical philosophy of Psychology, as it was formulated by Skinner. The changes, enhancements or alternatives to Skinner's criticism to internalism which were developed and proposed by other behavior analysts were not included. The conclusion synthesized above does not refer to the behavioral method as a methodology of research and psychotherapy. And that is a very important point. Indeed, the behavioral method's hypothetical successes in research and clinical practice have been used by the behaviorist community as favorable evidence to the validity of the criticism to internalism. Behavioral method results are used in comparison with those of the mentalist lines of thought for demonstrating the validity and objective accuracy of the first compared to the alleged explanatory fictions produced by the latter. The pragmatic argument is actually the most used by behavior analysts in defending the validity of Radical Behaviorism, and can be summarized as follows: Behavior analysis works, hence Radical Behaviorism's critical philosophy to Psychology is valid.

This is an invalid argument. The therapeutic methodology and the psychological theory it accompanies are two different theories. There is no strict relationship between the psychological and the methodological theories. The methodological theory establishes the assumptions to be followed in the determination of facts being analyzed. The psychological theory provides the assumptions which must be followed in the analysis itself, or in the interpretation of the facts revealed by the method application. Nothing prevents the facts revealed by the application of a methodology to be interpreted by the psychological theory of a different line of thought. It is thus possible, for instance, that the product of a behavior analysis receives a psychoanalytic interpretation.

Skinner's Radical Behaviorism does not provide us with a psychological theory. The psychological theory used by the behaviorist to interpret data revealed through the behavioral method is implicit in the analysis performed. However, an analyst's psychological theory is present in every behavior analysis he/she performs. It is this theory which makes analysis intelligible, it is this theory that gives it meaning. There will be no contradiction or objective hindrance if, instead of surreptitiously using an implicit psychological theory, the behavior analyst seeks for the meaning and intelligibility of his/her analysis in psychoanalytic theory. There will also be no contradiction or objective hindrance if the psychoanalyst seeks an existentialist interpretation, for instance, to the facts revealed through the application of psychoanalytic methodology.

The behavior analyst who uses the alleged successes of the behavioral method as evidence to the validity of Radical Behaviorism's critical philosophy to Psychology and for the subsequent refutation of the validity of all psychological or mentalist theory commits a fallacy. Psychological theories do not concern the revelation of facts, but their interpretation. If a behavior analyst believes that the behavioral method reveals fundamental facts in the explanation of behavior, facts which are obscured or go unnoticed in the application of competing methods, then his/her attack should be directed to these methods, not the psychological theories which accompany them. Radical Behaviorism's criticism should be directed to the psychoanalytic methodology, to the existentialist methodology, to the client-centered methodology, etc. In regards to this struggle, Radical Behaviorism has its arguments. As a methodology, behavior analysis has its strengths and weaknesses, and behavior analysts are fully justified in defending their working method. However, as a critical philosophy of Psychology and as a model of appropriate and objective language that conveys the precise sense of behavior and its causes, Radical Behaviorism is nothing more than a dead letter. Radical Behaviorism's philosophy is no longer relevant at all.

Radical Behaviorism, as a philosophy of Psychology, remains alive and debated among psychologists and psychology students because of the confusion that still exists between the validity of behavior analysis as a method and the validity of the criticism to internalism, the core of Radical Behaviorism, as a critical philosophy of Psychology. The correct distinction between Radical Behaviorism's practical and theoretical values should put its criticism to Psychology where it belongs: the shelf of dead philosophies.

REFERENCES

Skinner, B.F. (1953). *Science and Human Behavior.* New York: The Free Press.

Skinner, B.F. (1954). A Critique of Psychoanalytic Concepts and Theories, *Scientific Monthly. v. 79.* 300-305.

Skinner, B.F. (1971). *Beyond Freedom and Dignity*, Indianapolis: Hackett Publishing Company.